Mountain Blooms

Wildflowers of the Rockies

by

Millie

Johnson Books
Boulder

Thanks to ...

Sal King, Cyndi Nelson & Melinda Winegardner
    for your enthusiasm and outstanding art
    work that enabled the first book *Kinnikinnick*
    to happen way back in 1974.

Audrey Benedict for your expertise,
    your time, and your friendship.

David Johnson for introducing me to
    wildflowers and encouraging me to "be
    careful where you step." I wonder
    if you ever will decide which is your
    favorite flower?

Mira Perrizo, Associate Publisher at
    Johnson Books, for all your support,
    your patience, and your willingness
    to let me try some new ideas.

My family and all my caring friends ...

Back in the early '70s, when my puppy, Minka, and I first moved to Boulder, Cyndi and I shared an apartment. I had been looking for a little wildflower identification book to help me as I explored these new things called "the Rockies." I could only find books that told me much more than I wanted to know.

I mentioned to Cyndi that I had this idea for a wildflower book. Her response was "Do it." I shook my head. "I'll help you!" she said. And so we did.

We have worked together on books for over 25 years now. Along the way, I introduced her to her husband, Scott, and they had 4 glorious children. But still we spent hours and days and weeks together working, laughing, crying, traveling, and celebrating. Now she wants to move on to the many other things in her life and has been brave enough to let me strike out on my own ... at least for a while.

These wildflowers
are dedicated to

Cyndi

for a friendship
that goes beyond
all understanding.

How to use this flower guide ...

Head for the hills — with this book in your back pocket and a friend or puppy by your side. Any trail will do. Walk with care ... wildflowers are everywhere.

For most hikers, the fun in identifying wildflowers is being able to make a close identification, not a botanical one. So if you find a little flower that looks just like ... say the penstemon in this book but it's a different color and has a different leaf, at least you know you've identified a penstemon. Be proud.

Remember that some flowers go by many names, some are in the same family but have different leaves or colors, some even vary a lot as the seasons change. Scores of flowers seem to be everywhere, a handful hide in very special places. Many are along the road, others will fill a meadow just over the hill, and a few you may see just once in a lifetime. Flowers are a mountain adventure. Tho you dasn't pick 'em, you can always carry them away in your mind's eye or in your camera's eye.

This book was designed to be self-explanatory and easy to use. For each flower you will find:

a common name (in **bold italics**)
a family name (in *italics*)
a scientific name
the approximate size
the usual months it can be found.

Hoping you and the wildflowers
enjoy each other, *Millie*

State flower
of Nevada
Artemisia
tridentata

Aster Family

Aug. thru Sept.

2 – 4′

Sagebrush

Aromatic
silver-green shrub
with a shedding bark.
Prefers well-drained places.
Helps hide the nests of
many small animals.

For up to 60 years,
this monumental plant stores
energy in its roots.
Finally, it sends up a tall
stalk that blooms but once.
Purple flecks dot the
greenish flowers.
Dry stems can last years.
Often found in meadows
and with sagebrush.

May thru Aug.

4 – 6′

Frasera speciosa

*Gentian
Family*

Monument Plant

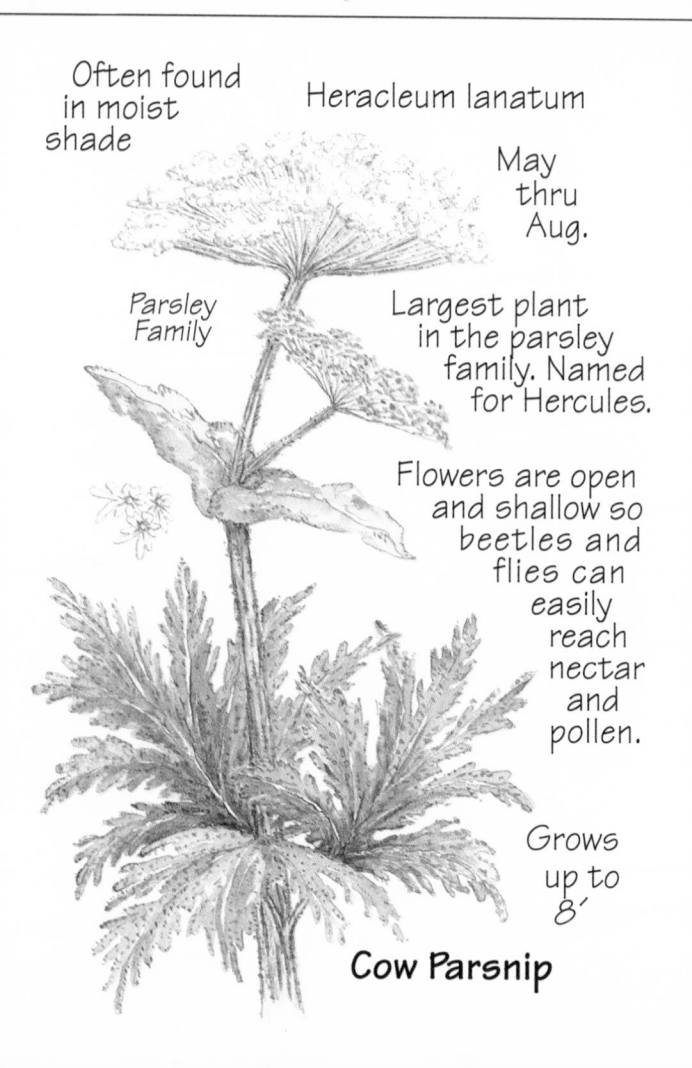

Often found
in moist
shade

Heracleum lanatum

May
thru
Aug.

*Parsley
Family*

Largest plant
in the parsley
family. Named
for Hercules.

Flowers are open
and shallow so
beetles and
flies can
easily
reach
nectar
and
pollen.

Grows
up to
8´

Cow Parsnip

Achilles discovered
its healing
properties, and
used it as medicine
to heal his soldiers'
wounds.

Achillea
lanulosa

Yarrow

Aster Family

Widely
distributed

1 – 3′

May
thru
Sept.

Queen Anne's Lace

Daucus carota

May have a central purple
flower. Ancestor of the
cultivated carrot.
Often seen on
roadsides or other
weedy sites.

*Parsley
Family*

1 – 4′

May thru
Sept.

Thimbleberry

2 – 6'

Oreobatus deliciosus

A shrub of moist sunny places. Has large leaves similar to a maple. Resembles wild raspberry but lacks prickles on the stem.

Rose Family

May thru July

12 – 20"
March thru June

Early spring flower with almost invisible slender stalk. From a distance, looks like a sprinkling of stars. Companion of sagebrush.

Lithophragma parviflorum

Saxifrage Family

Starflower

A sweet-smelling bloom that opens at dusk. Found in shrublands, especially near ant hills. Ages purplish. Pollinated by night-flying moths.

April thru Sept.

Evening Primrose Family

Oenothera caespitosa

Stemless Evening Primrose

1 – 8"

Philadelphus lewisii

May thru July

"Mock Orange" smells like orange blossoms. Idaho's state flower. Likes rocky slopes.

Hydrangea Family

Shrub 4 – 10'

Syringa

Amelanchier alnifolia

Often found on dry slopes.

April thru Aug.

Rose Family

Important food for birds & other wildlife. Indians used berries in pemmican.

Serviceberry

Shrub 4 – 30'

Look low in moist open sites. May thru August. A treat eaten by many animals.

Rose Family

2 – 4"

Fragaria virginiana

Strawberry

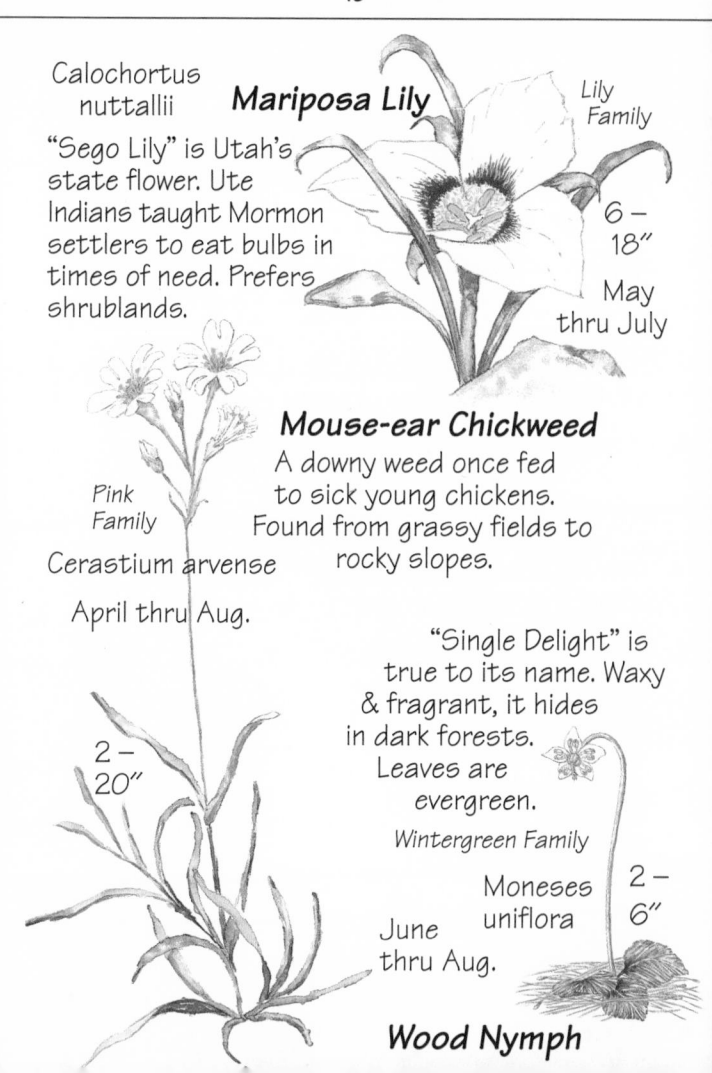

Calochortus nuttallii

Mariposa Lily

Lily Family

"Sego Lily" is Utah's state flower. Ute Indians taught Mormon settlers to eat bulbs in times of need. Prefers shrublands.

6 – 18"

May thru July

Mouse-ear Chickweed

A downy weed once fed to sick young chickens. Found from grassy fields to rocky slopes.

Pink Family

Cerastium arvense

April thru Aug.

2 – 20"

"Single Delight" is true to its name. Waxy & fragrant, it hides in dark forests. Leaves are evergreen.

Wintergreen Family

Moneses uniflora

2 – 6"

June thru Aug.

Wood Nymph

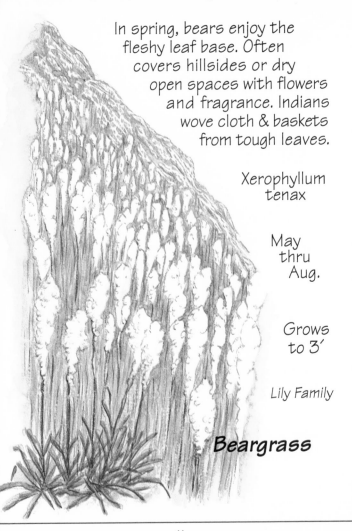

In spring, bears enjoy the fleshy leaf base. Often covers hillsides or dry open spaces with flowers and fragrance. Indians wove cloth & baskets from tough leaves.

Xerophyllum tenax

May thru Aug.

Grows to 3'

Lily Family

Beargrass

Heather

Heath Family

Cassiope mertensiana

Heather often called "Heath."
This little chimer forms
mats above timberline.

July thru Aug.

2 – 12"

Sandwort

Arenaria fendleri

Pink
Family

Many varieties grow from plains
to alpine. Also known as
"Sandywinks," prefers sandy
well-drained soil.

2 – 12"

June
thru
Aug.

Leucocrinum montanum

A low and fragrant early
bloom of foothill meadows.
Announces spring.

April thru June

Lily
Family

1 – 8"

Sand Lily

Evergreen leaves are an important food for ptarmigan. Large patches common on high alpine slopes. Hardy & adaptive, hugs the ground for warmth and wind protection.

Rose Family

2 – 10"

Dryad

June thru Aug.

Dryas octopetala

Buttercup Family

Has a global shape. Opens soon after snow melts. Happy in high wet meadows & near streambanks.

Trollius laxus

4 – 20"

Globeflower

May thru Aug.

1 – 8"

Marsh Marigold

Caltha leptosepala

May thru Aug.

Buttercup Family

Pushes up thru melting snow. Flowers open in just 2 days. Often found in wet places with Globeflower.

Grows to 3' with dense clusters of flowers.

Has dark large leaves.

Smilacina racemosa

"Solomon's Seal" has fewer flowers & grows to 6." Has light skinny leaves.

Wild Lily of the Valley

False Solomon's Seal

Smilacina stellata

Both in Lily family, like moist shade & bloom May thru July.

8 – 36"   June thru Sept.

A woolly little cluster of pearls often found along trails. Dry flower stalks are long lasting.

Anaphalis margaritacea

Pearly Everlasting   Aster Family

Heath Family

Kinnikinnick

Arctostaphylos uva-ursi

1 – 6"   March thru June

Widespread creeper with evergreen leaves found in open forests. Known as "Bearberry."

Saxifraga
rhomboidea

Widespread on open moist
slopes. Flowers form a dense
round head.

Polygonum bistortoides

*Buckwheat
Family*

May
thru
Aug.

Snowball

*Saxifrage
Family*

2 – 12"

May
thru
Aug.

8 – 28"

A sweet-
smelling mat
of the tundra,
often found with
Moss Campion &
Forget-me-nots.

*Phlox
Family*

8 – 12"

May
thru
July

American Bistort

Phlox

Phlox multiflora

Can sometimes
blanket a wet meadow.
A delicacy for wildlife.

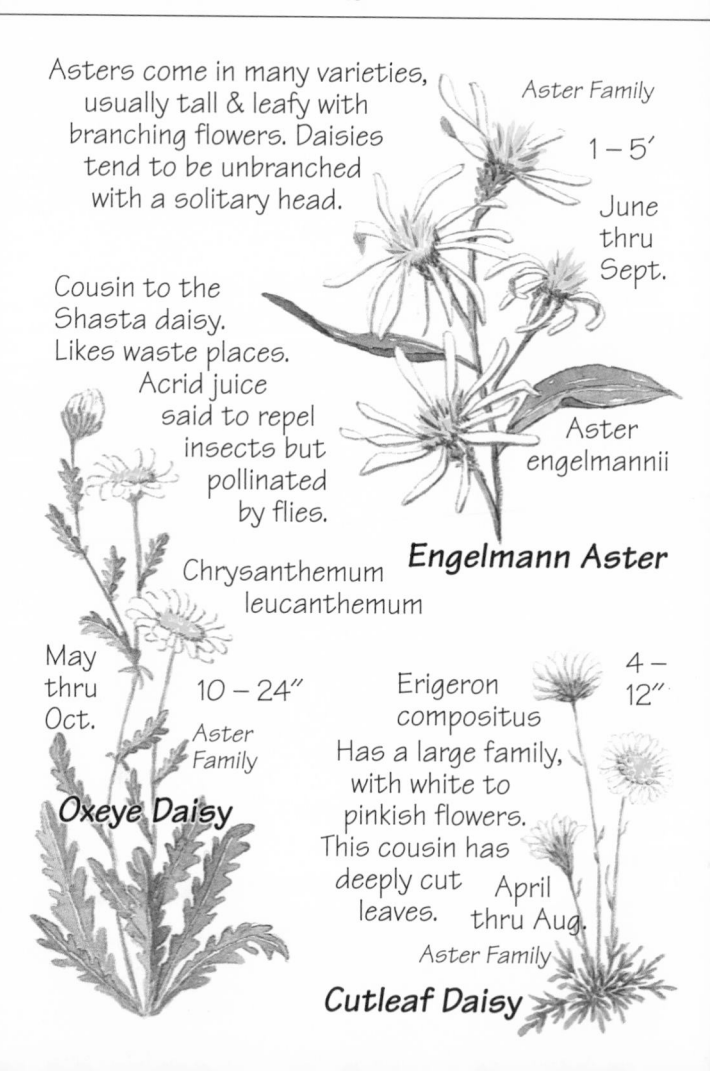

Asters come in many varieties, usually tall & leafy with branching flowers. Daisies tend to be unbranched with a solitary head.

Aster Family

1 – 5'

June thru Sept.

Cousin to the Shasta daisy. Likes waste places. Acrid juice said to repel insects but pollinated by flies.

Aster engelmannii

Engelmann Aster

Chrysanthemum leucanthemum

May thru Oct.

10 – 24"

Aster Family

Oxeye Daisy

Erigeron compositus

Has a large family, with white to pinkish flowers. This cousin has deeply cut leaves.

April thru Aug.

4 – 12"

Aster Family

Cutleaf Daisy

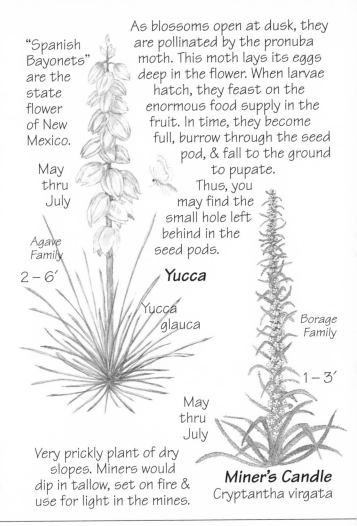

"Spanish Bayonets" are the state flower of New Mexico.

May thru July

Agave Family

2 – 6′

As blossoms open at dusk, they are pollinated by the pronuba moth. This moth lays its eggs deep in the flower. When larvae hatch, they feast on the enormous food supply in the fruit. In time, they become full, burrow through the seed pod, & fall to the ground to pupate.

Thus, you may find the small hole left behind in the seed pods.

Yucca

Yucca glauca

Very prickly plant of dry slopes. Miners would dip in tallow, set on fire & use for light in the mines.

Borage Family

1 – 3′

May thru July

Miner's Candle
Cryptantha virgata

Argemone polyanthemos

April thru June   *Poppy Family*

Many cousins in yellow, pink
or lavender. Very poisonous.
Animals avoid because so
prickly & distasteful.
Brightens disturbed
places.

1 – 3'

Prickly Poppy

*Plantain
Family*
2 – 16"

"Planta"
is Latin for "sole of the foot."
Leaves resemble footprints.
Often found in waste areas.

Plantago major

Plantain   June thru
Oct.

"Wakerobin" blooms early
along streambanks or in
the deep wood. Turns
pinkish with age.

Feb.
thru
June

4 –
16"

Trillium   *Lily Family*
ovatum
Trillium

A common colonizer
of dry areas.
Many varieties.
Has hairy leaves
that feel silky.

Aster Family

Heterotheca villosa

Golden Aster

May thru Oct.
8 – 20"

Comes in many colors.
Blossoms are waxy,
which helps prevent
evaporation of
stored water.
Flowers last only
a day or two. Often
found in shrublands.

3 – 6"

May thru July

*Cactus
Family*

Opuntia
polyacantha

Prickly Pear Cactus

Called "Toadflax" as it looks a bit like a   2 – 4´
toad with leaves like a flax. Found at
lower elevations near campsites,
mines, trails, or waste places.

June
thru
Sept.

"Golden Banner"
frequently
brightens
disturbed
areas.
May thru
Aug.

Linaria
vulgaris   *Figwort
                            Family*

Butter and Eggs

Thermopsis
montana
*Pea
Family*   1 – 4´

Golden Pea

Very
poisonous.

Monkey-
flower

March
thru
Sept.

Mimulus
1 – 2´   guttatus

A large family, all with little
monkey faces. Comes in a variety
of colors. Likes any place wet.

*Figwort
Family*

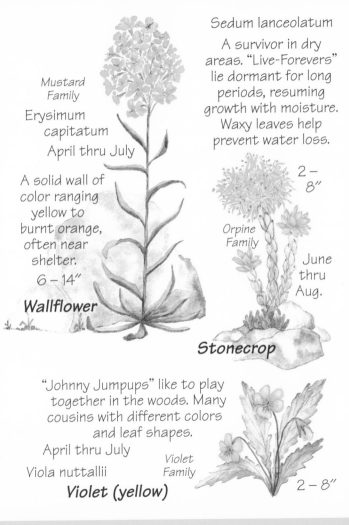

Mustard
Family

Erysimum
capitatum

April thru July

A solid wall of
color ranging
yellow to
burnt orange,
often near
shelter.

6 – 14"

Wallflower

Sedum lanceolatum

A survivor in dry
areas. "Live-Forevers"
lie dormant for long
periods, resuming
growth with moisture.
Waxy leaves help
prevent water loss.

2 –
8"

Orpine
Family

June
thru
Aug.

Stonecrop

"Johnny Jumpups" like to play
together in the woods. Many
cousins with different colors
and leaf shapes.

April thru July

Viola nuttallii

Violet
Family

Violet (yellow)

2 – 8"

Ratibida columnifera

Aster Family

A bloom of the low mountains, often seen in gravelly areas, along roads or railways.

July thru Sept.

1 – 3´

Coneflower

Common from the Rockies to the East Coast. Solitary flower on a hairy stem.

Aster Family

3 – 4´

June thru Sept.

Common Sunflower

Helianthus annuus

Flat center button follows sun east to west thru the day. Likes disturbed areas.

1 – 3´

Aster Family

June thru Aug.

Rudbeckia hirta

Blackeyed Susan

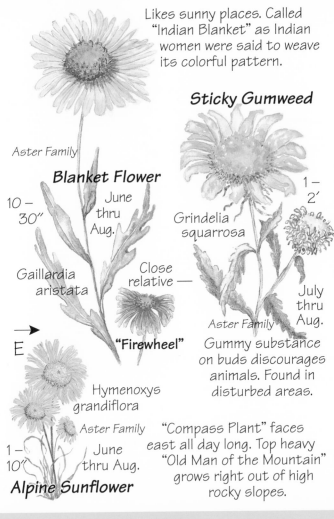

Likes sunny places. Called "Indian Blanket" as Indian women were said to weave its colorful pattern.

Sticky Gumweed

Aster Family

Blanket Flower

June thru Aug.

10 – 30″

1 – 2′

Grindelia squarrosa

Gaillardia aristata

Close relative —

July thru Aug.

Aster Family

"Firewheel"

Gummy substance on buds discourages animals. Found in disturbed areas.

E

Hymenoxys grandiflora

Aster Family

June thru Aug.

1 – 10″

Alpine Sunflower

"Compass Plant" faces east all day long. Top heavy "Old Man of the Mountain" grows right out of high rocky slopes.

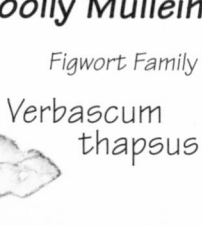

Has a
two year
life cycle ... first
to form a ground-
hugging rosette
of leaves and
second, to grow a
long stem. Flowers
bloom a few at a
time. Leaves
are covered with
hairs, feel like
velvet, and
make excellent
toilet paper.

June
thru
Aug.

2 – 7′

Woolly Mullein

Figwort Family

Verbascum
thapsus

Mule's Ears

Aster Family

Wyethia amplexicaulis

Leaves look like mule's ears growing along the stem. They are glossy & hairless. Likes moist meadows.

May thru June
12 – 32"

Hairy, arrow-shaped leaves cluster at base of flower, not on stalk. Likes sagebrush country.

8 – 32"
Balsamorhiza sagittata
May thru June

Aster Family

Arrowleaf Balsamroot

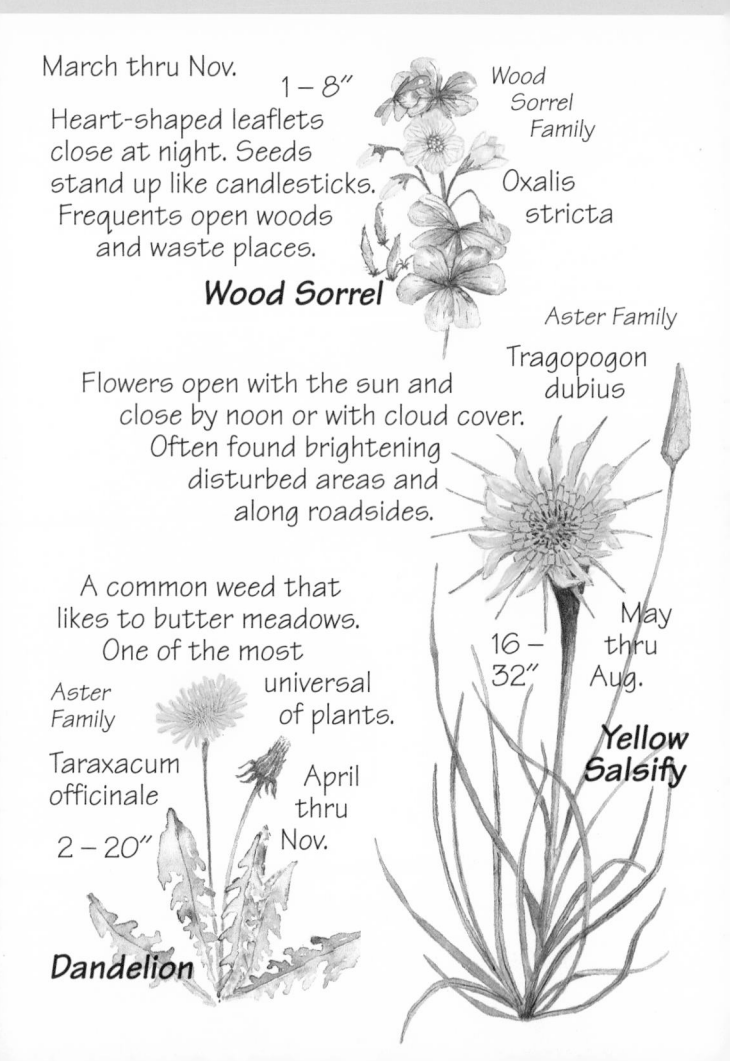

March thru Nov.

1 – 8″

Wood Sorrel Family

Heart-shaped leaflets close at night. Seeds stand up like candlesticks. Frequents open woods and waste places.

Oxalis stricta

Wood Sorrel

Aster Family

Tragopogon dubius

Flowers open with the sun and close by noon or with cloud cover. Often found brightening disturbed areas and along roadsides.

A common weed that likes to butter meadows. One of the most universal of plants.

16 – 32″

May thru Aug.

Aster Family

Yellow Salsify

Taraxacum officinale

April thru Nov.

2 – 20″

Dandelion

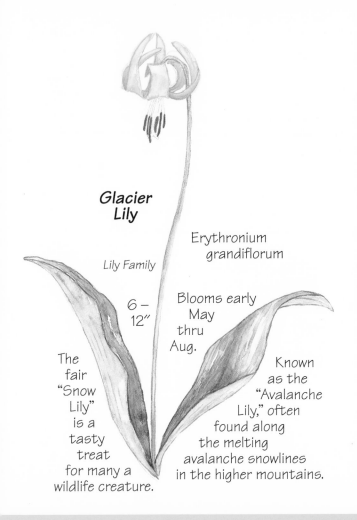

Glacier Lily

Lily Family

Erythronium grandiflorum

6 – 12"

Blooms early May thru Aug.

The fair "Snow Lily" is a tasty treat for many a wildlife creature.

Known as the "Avalanche Lily," often found along the melting avalanche snowlines in the higher mountains.

Rabbitbrush
Aster Family

A deciduous shrub that thrives where too dry for other plants to survive. Colonizes disturbed areas.

Chrysothamnus nauseosus

1 – 7′

Aug. thru Oct.

From a large variable family. Little yellow cups turn pinkish in the fall. Flowers branch from stalk like an umbrella. Prefers dry places.

June thru Aug.

Buckwheat Family

Sulphur Flower

Eriogonum umbellatum

4 – 12″

An early bloomer near sagebrush. Also known as "Bashful Fritillaria." Grows rusty or purplish with age. Grazed by many wild animals.

Lily Family

Yellow Bell

4 – 12″

Fritillaria pudica

March thru June

Cinquefoil

Shrub to 36"

June thru Aug.

Potentilla fruticosa

Rose Family

Many cousins. This one is a widespread hardy shrub. Game animals graze on leaves all winter.

June thru Aug.

4 – 12"

A waxy bloom that pushes up through the snow in high mountain meadows.

Ranunculus adoneus

Buttercup Family

Alpine Buttercup

In fall, holly-like leaves turn color.

Mahonia repens

Barberry Family

May thru June

4 – 8"

A low creeper found in open pine forests. State flower of Oregon.

Oregon Grape

29

Over 100 species in the West ... about 3,000 species worldwide. Found in moist areas.

June thru Sept.

2 – 5′

Aster Family

Senecio triangularis

Arrowleaf Groundsel

1 – 5′

Aster Family

Many species of Goldenrod. Pollen are too heavy to wind pollinate. Ragweed usually the hay fever culprit. Likes wet meadows.

July thru Sept.

Solidago canadensis

Goldenrod

Matted hairs cover stems & leaves. This reduces water loss so plant can survive in dry places.

Aster Family   4 – 24″

Eriophyllum lanatum

May thru July

Woolly Yellow Daisy

April thru May

Lewisia pygmaea

Resembles Bitterroot but flowers are smaller. Leaves are longer and stay green thru blooming.

2 – 4"

Lewisia

Purslane Family

2 – 4"

June thru Sept.

Linnaea borealis

Honeysuckle Family

Twin Flower

Bitterroot first noted by Meriwether Lewis in 1806 when he & Clark explored what is now called the Bitterroot Valley. There are also Bitterroot Mountains & a Bitterroot River. Leaves die back as flowers appear.

Montana state flower.

Lewisia rediviva

1 – 2"

Bitterroot

Purslane Family

May thru July

Delicate ground cover in moist conifer woods. Fragrant, especially near evening.

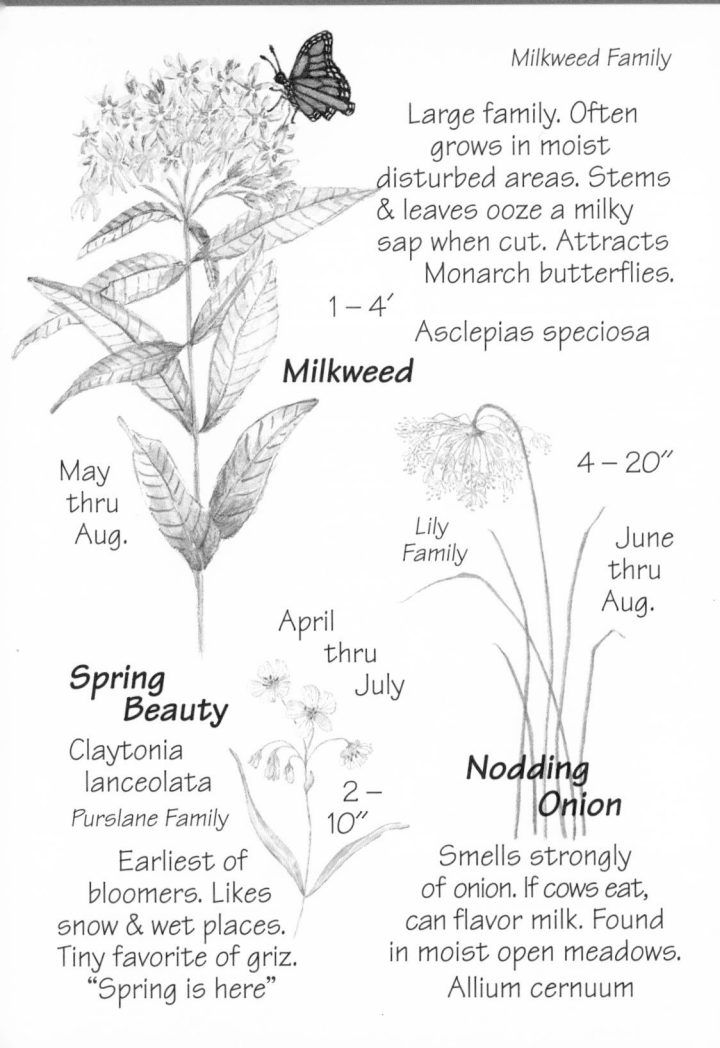

Milkweed Family

Large family. Often grows in moist disturbed areas. Stems & leaves ooze a milky sap when cut. Attracts Monarch butterflies.

1 – 4'

Asclepias speciosa

Milkweed

May thru Aug.

4 – 20"

Lily Family

June thru Aug.

April thru July

Spring Beauty

Claytonia lanceolata
Purslane Family

2 – 10"

Nodding Onion

Earliest of bloomers. Likes snow & wet places. Tiny favorite of griz. "Spring is here"

Smells strongly of onion. If cows eat, can flavor milk. Found in moist open meadows.

Allium cernuum

Anthers are tucked into little hollows on the petals. These spring forward with any insect motion, leaving pollen on the intruder who takes it to the next flower.

Bog Laurel

Kalmia microphylla

June thru Sept.

4 – 15"

Heath Family

Heath Family

4 – 16"

Heath

Phyllodoce empetriformis

This dwarf evergreen shrub makes a dense ground cover near or above timberline.

June thru Aug.

A tundra "cushion plant" often found with Phlox and Forget-me-nots.

Pink Family

1 – 3"

Moss Campion

June thru Aug.

Silene acaulis

A sweet-scented ancestor
of the domestic rose.
The fruit or "rose hips"
are eaten by birds thru
the winter. A shrub,
often found along streams.

Wild Rose

Rosa woodsii
June thru Aug.   4 – 6'

Rose
Family

Pea
Family

1 – 3'

Red Clover

Trifolium pratense
June thru Aug.

St. Patrick is said to
have chosen the
clover leaf as a
symbol of the
Holy Trinity.

Common in
disturbed soil.

June thru Aug.

"Queen's Crown" comes from
a large royal family of
succulent plants. Often
found by high streams or
at the edges of marshes.

Stonecrop
Family

Clementsia
rhodantha

1 – 12"

Rose Crown

Smells like a goat but bees
like the nectar. Grows in
disturbed locales.

Caper
Family

1 – 5′

June thru Sept.

Bee Plant

Cleome
serrulata

Carduus
nutans

Aster Family

1 –
9′

A weed of dry
waste areas.
Head nods to
side. Attracts
butterflies.
June
thru
Oct.

Bull Thistle

Aster Family

Musk
Thistle

Cirsium
vulgare

1 –
6′

Very showy and very prickly.
Common in pastures & disturbed
places. Thistledown makes good
tinder to start a fire.

July thru Sept.

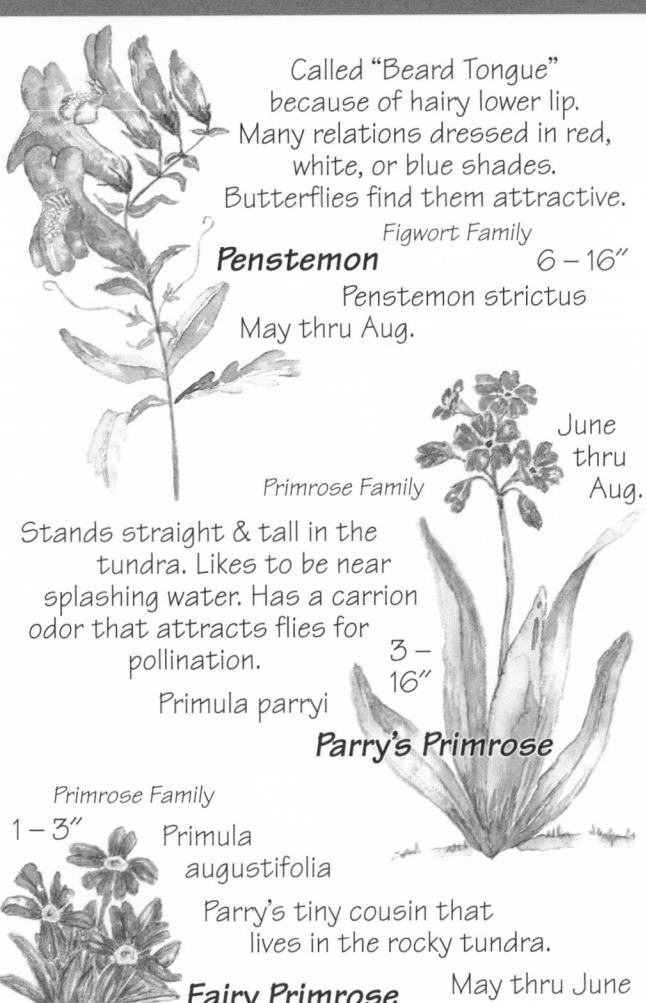

Called "Beard Tongue"
because of hairy lower lip.
Many relations dressed in red,
white, or blue shades.
Butterflies find them attractive.

Figwort Family

Penstemon 6 – 16"

Penstemon strictus

May thru Aug.

June
thru
Aug.

Primrose Family

Stands straight & tall in the
tundra. Likes to be near
splashing water. Has a carrion
odor that attracts flies for
pollination.

3 –
16"

Primula parryi

Parry's Primrose

Primrose Family

1 – 3" Primula
augustifolia

Parry's tiny cousin that
lives in the rocky tundra.

Fairy Primrose May thru June

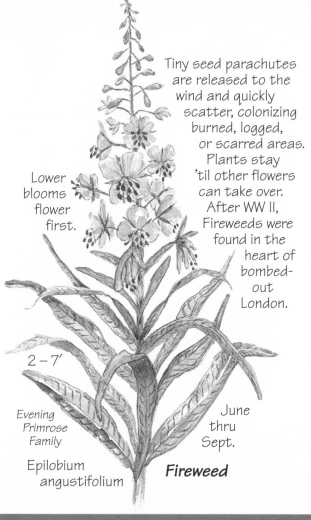

Tiny seed parachutes
are released to the
wind and quickly
scatter, colonizing
burned, logged,
or scarred areas.
Plants stay
'til other flowers
can take over.
After WW II,
Fireweeds were
found in the
heart of
bombed-
out
London.

Lower
blooms
flower
first.

2 – 7'

*Evening
Primrose
Family*

*Epilobium
angustifolium*

June
thru
Sept.

Fireweed

Lives 2 years, establishes a rosette of leaves,
then develops the stem and flowers.
A favorite of hummers who go deep into flowers
for nectar while gathering pollen on their heads
to take to the next plant.
Often found with sage-
brush.

Ipomopsis
aggregata

1 – 3'

Has a
skunky
odor when
crushed.

Broadtailed
Hummingbird

Also
attracts
hummers.
Likes
dry,
rocky
places.

May
thru
June

Phlox
Family

Penstemon
eatonii

May
thru
Sept.

Firecracker

Figwort
Family

15 –
24"

Scarlet Gilia

Wyoming state flower.

Adds color to pinon / juniper woodlands & sage. Comes in white, yellow and all shades of red.

Little Red Elephants

Figwort Family

June thru Aug.

May thru Sept.

Figwort Family
4 – 16"

Indian Paintbrush

Castilleja linariaefolia

Lilium philadelphicum
1 – 2'

Lily Family

June thru Aug.

Was once very common. Graces meadows and aspen groves. Wilts quickly when picked.

Wood Lily

You'll smile when you see it. Grazed by elk in wet meadows. Fernlike leaves.

Pedicularis groenlandica
1 – 28"

Known as "Prairie Smoke" because of long feathery seeds. Flowers hang their heads as seeds sail away on the breeze. Leaves are fern-like. Often found in coniferous woods.

Rose Family

6 – 24"

Geum triflorum

Old Man's Whiskers

April thru Aug.

Starry host often gathers in moist meadows & at streamsides. Pollen released to the wind by the buzzing vibrations of bees.

Shooting Star

Primrose Family

April thru Aug.

Dodecatheon pulchellum

4 – 24"

Sorrel

Oxyria digyna

Buckwheat Family

1 – 10"

July thru Sept.

Forms communities in high rocky places. The reddish-winged fruit is most conspicuous. Leaves heart shaped.

Leafy Aster

Aster Family

8 – 20"

July thru Sept.

Aster foliaceus apricus

Asters are related to **Daisies**

- bloom in fall
- taller
- several flowers per stalk

- in spring
- shorter
- often lone flower per stalk

and aster petals overlap like shingles.

Corallorhiza maculata

Pinedrops

June thru Aug.

Pinesap Family

Pterospora andromedea

1 – 3'

Coralroot

April thru Sept.

Orchid Family

8 – 18"

Both hide in the shade of conifer forests.

Known as saprophytes, these plants do not have leaves & do not photosynthesize. They get their food from the organic debris of the forest floor.

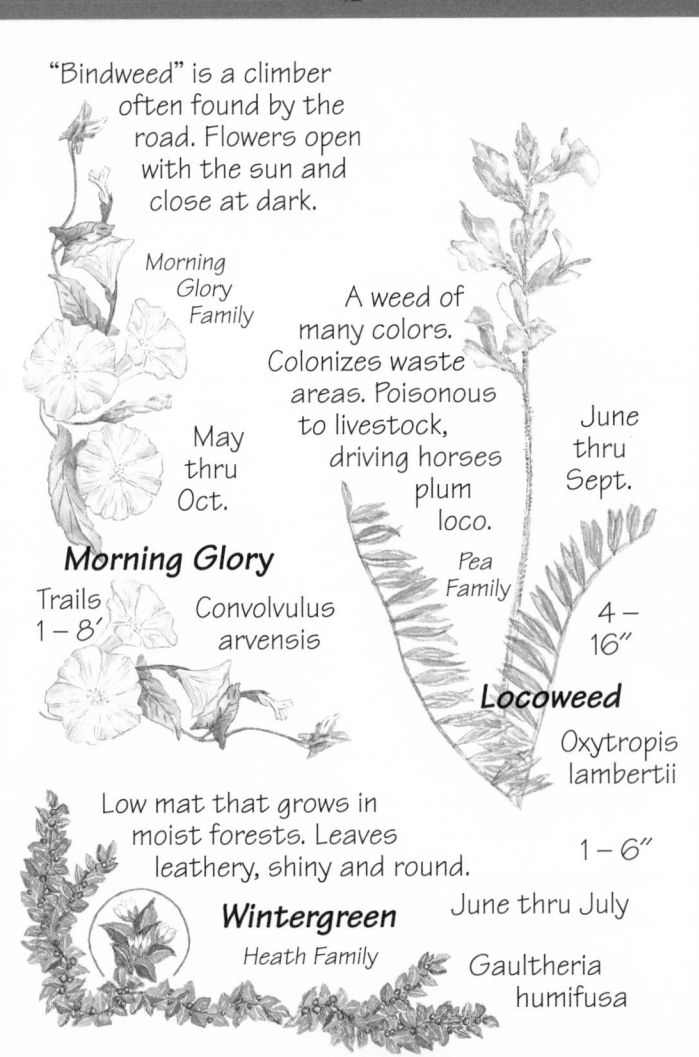

"Bindweed" is a climber often found by the road. Flowers open with the sun and close at dark.

Morning Glory Family

A weed of many colors. Colonizes waste areas. Poisonous to livestock, driving horses plum loco.

Pea Family

May thru Oct.

June thru Sept.

Morning Glory

Trails 1 – 8'

Convolvulus arvensis

4 – 16"

Locoweed

Oxytropis lambertii

Low mat that grows in moist forests. Leaves leathery, shiny and round.

1 – 6"

Wintergreen

Heath Family

June thru July

Gaultheria humifusa

Calypso bulbosa
Orchid Family
2 – 8"

March thru July

A rare find. Hides deep in old shady forests. Likes a rich mossy palace. Has a single leaf.

Fairy Slipper

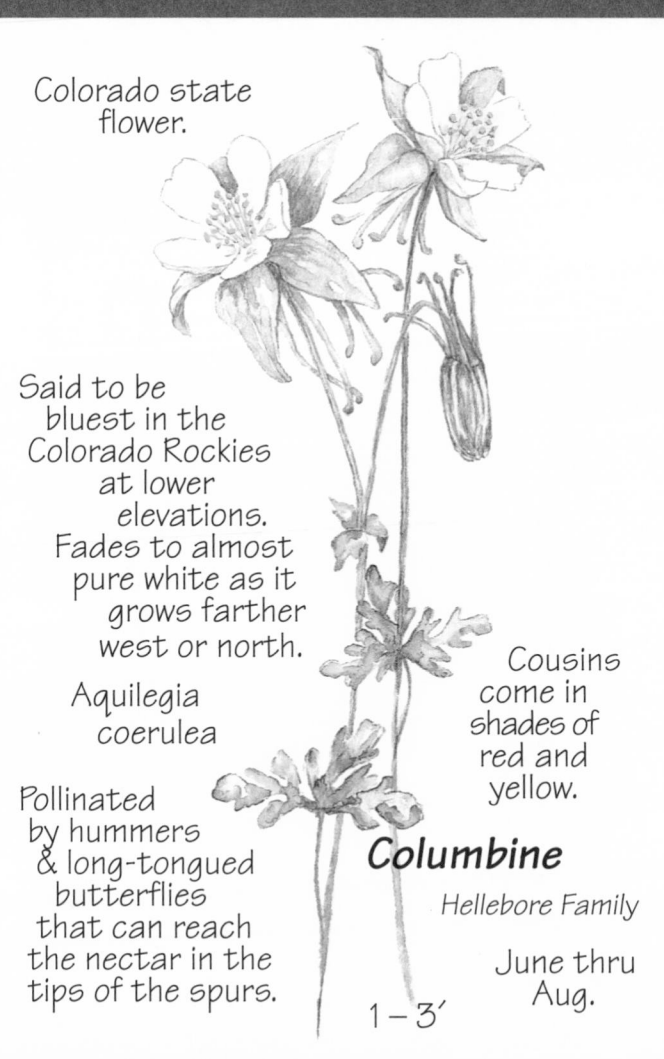

Colorado state
  flower.

Said to be
  bluest in the
  Colorado Rockies
    at lower
    elevations.
  Fades to almost
    pure white as it
    grows farther
    west or north.

  Aquilegia
    coerulea

Pollinated
  by hummers
  & long-tongued
    butterflies
    that can reach
    the nectar in the
    tips of the spurs.

Cousins
  come in
  shades of
    red and
    yellow.

Columbine

Hellebore Family

June thru
  Aug.

1 – 3′

Leaves look like steps of a ladder.
Has a skunky smell when stepped on.
Polemonium   Likes high altitudes.
  pulcherrimum

Phlox Family

1 – 8"

Jacob's Ladder

June thru Aug.

Very poisonous.
A European cousin
  once used as
  wolf bait.
Thus, "Wolfbane"
  part of
  werewolf
  lore.

Aconitum
  columbianum

Hellebore Family

Lupine

Lupinus
  sp.

June thru Aug.

1 – 4'

Monkshood

May
thru
Aug.

Often found in
  aspen forests.

Pea Family

The state
  flower of Texas,
    known as "Bluebonnets."
      Has about 600 relatives in
        North America. After a rain,
          holds droplets of water   1 – 2'
            in center of its leaves.

Legend tells of a lad picking these riverside flowers for his betrothed. Alas! He slipped & fell into the torrent but threw the flowers to his love shouting "Forget-me-not" as he was swept away.

State flower of Alaska.

May thru Aug.

Myosotis alpestris
Borage Family

Forget-me-not

4 – 12"

A cushion of the tundra often found with Phlox and Moss Campion.

Borage Family

1 – 4"

Alpine Forget-me-not

Eritrichium nanum

June thru Aug.

Grows in waste areas.

Chicory

Aster Family

March thru Oct.

1 – 6'

Spread from the Mediterranean throughout the world due to the love of its roots, which are roasted, ground & added to coffee.

Cichorium intybus

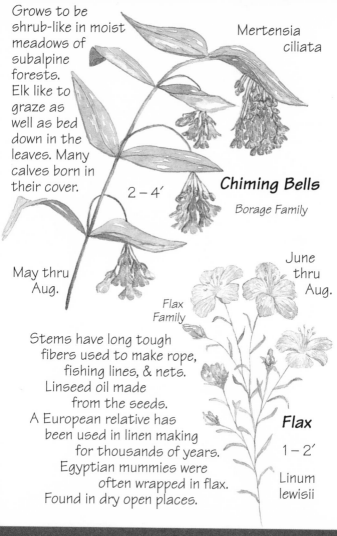

Grows to be shrub-like in moist meadows of subalpine forests. Elk like to graze as well as bed down in the leaves. Many calves born in their cover.

Mertensia ciliata

2 – 4′

Chiming Bells

Borage Family

May thru Aug.

Flax Family

June thru Aug.

Stems have long tough fibers used to make rope, fishing lines, & nets. Linseed oil made from the seeds. A European relative has been used in linen making for thousands of years. Egyptian mummies were often wrapped in flax. Found in dry open places.

Flax

1 – 2′

Linum lewisii

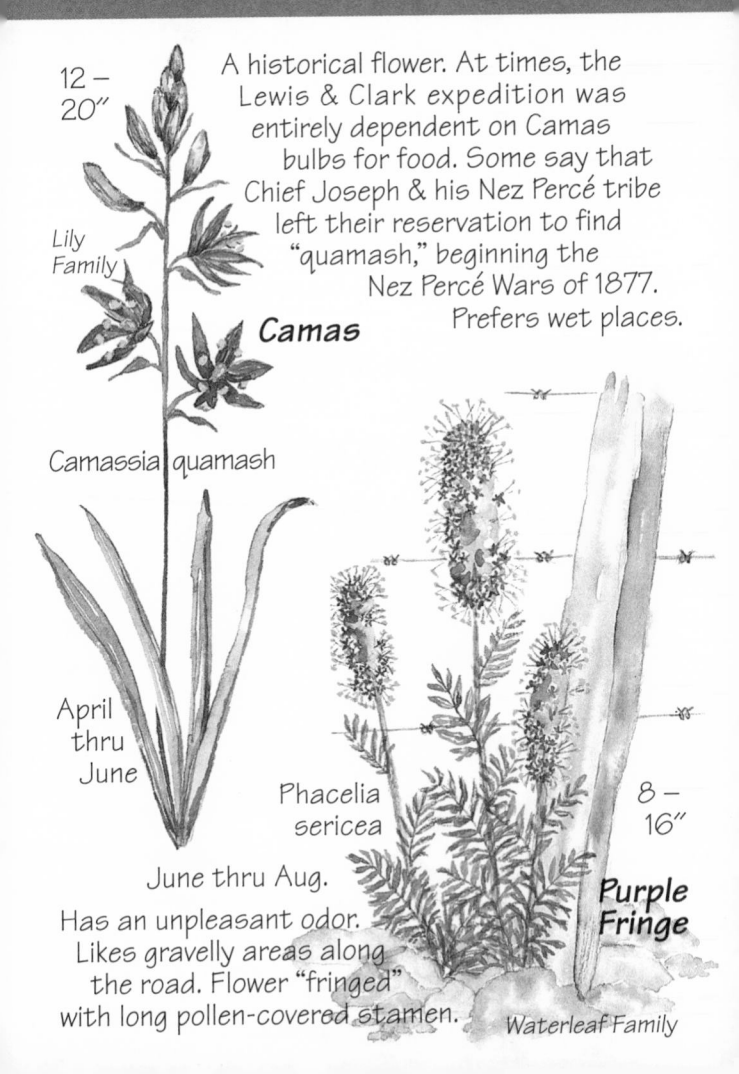

12 – 20"

Lily Family

A historical flower. At times, the Lewis & Clark expedition was entirely dependent on Camas bulbs for food. Some say that Chief Joseph & his Nez Percé tribe left their reservation to find "quamash," beginning the Nez Percé Wars of 1877. Prefers wet places.

Camas

Camassia quamash

April thru June

Phacelia sericea

8 – 16"

June thru Aug.

Has an unpleasant odor. Likes gravelly areas along the road. Flower "fringed" with long pollen-covered stamen.

Purple Fringe

Waterleaf Family

July thru Oct.

2 – 12"

Gentian

Gentiana calycosa

Gentian Family

Opens but a short time each day. Cousins found in wet places in the Himalayas, the Andes, and the Alps.

Sky Pilot

4 – 16"

Named because it lives so high up in the rocky tundra.

Has a skunky smell when stepped on.

Phlox Family

Polemonium viscosum

June thru Aug.

Showy Fleabane

Erigeron speciosus

June thru Sept.

Aster Family

6 – 30"

Likes open woods. Has more than 50 narrow petals. Can look tired even when it first comes into flower.

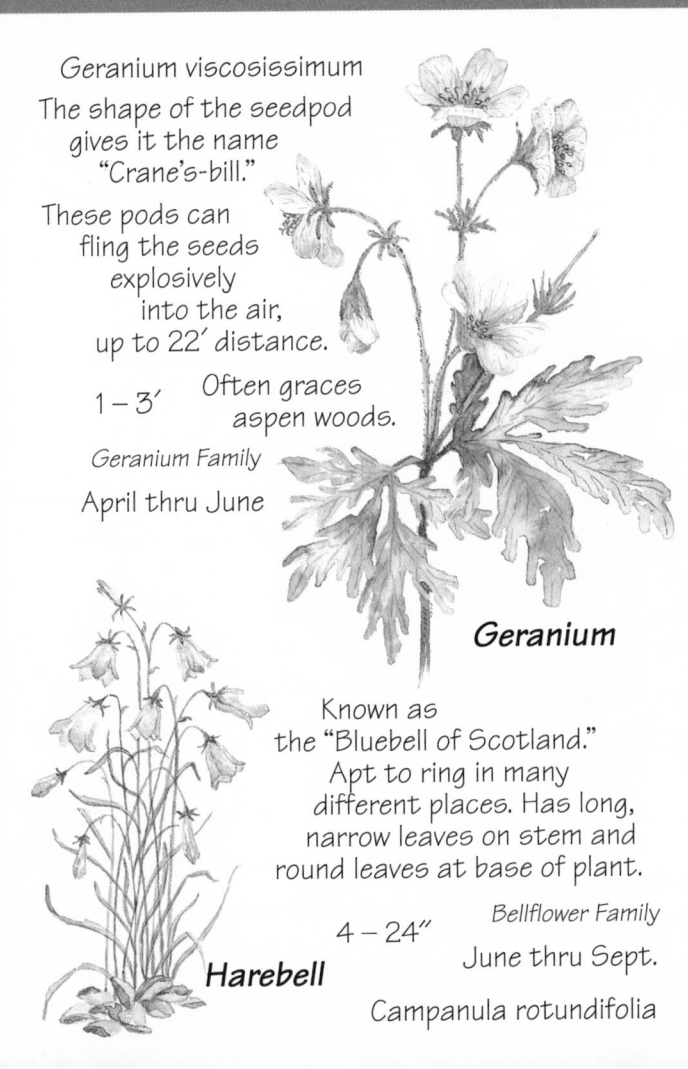

Geranium viscosissimum

The shape of the seedpod gives it the name "Crane's-bill."

These pods can fling the seeds explosively into the air, up to 22' distance.

1 – 3' Often graces aspen woods.

Geranium Family

April thru June

Geranium

Known as the "Bluebell of Scotland." Apt to ring in many different places. Has long, narrow leaves on stem and round leaves at base of plant.

4 – 24" *Bellflower Family*

Harebell June thru Sept.

Campanula rotundifolia

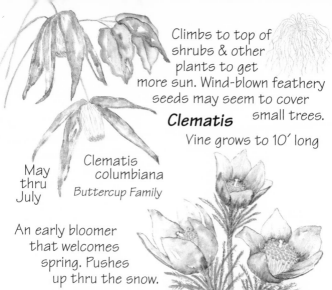

Climbs to top of shrubs & other plants to get more sun. Wind-blown feathery seeds may seem to cover small trees.

Clematis

Vine grows to 10′ long

May thru July

Clematis columbiana

Buttercup Family

An early bloomer that welcomes spring. Pushes up thru the snow.

1 – 14″   May thru Aug.

Buttercup Family   **Pasque**

Anemone patens

Viola adunca

April thru Aug.   1 – 4″

About 900 species worldwide with different colors & leaves. This one likes moist meadows & glades and has a heart-shaped leaf.

Violet (blue)   *Violet Family*

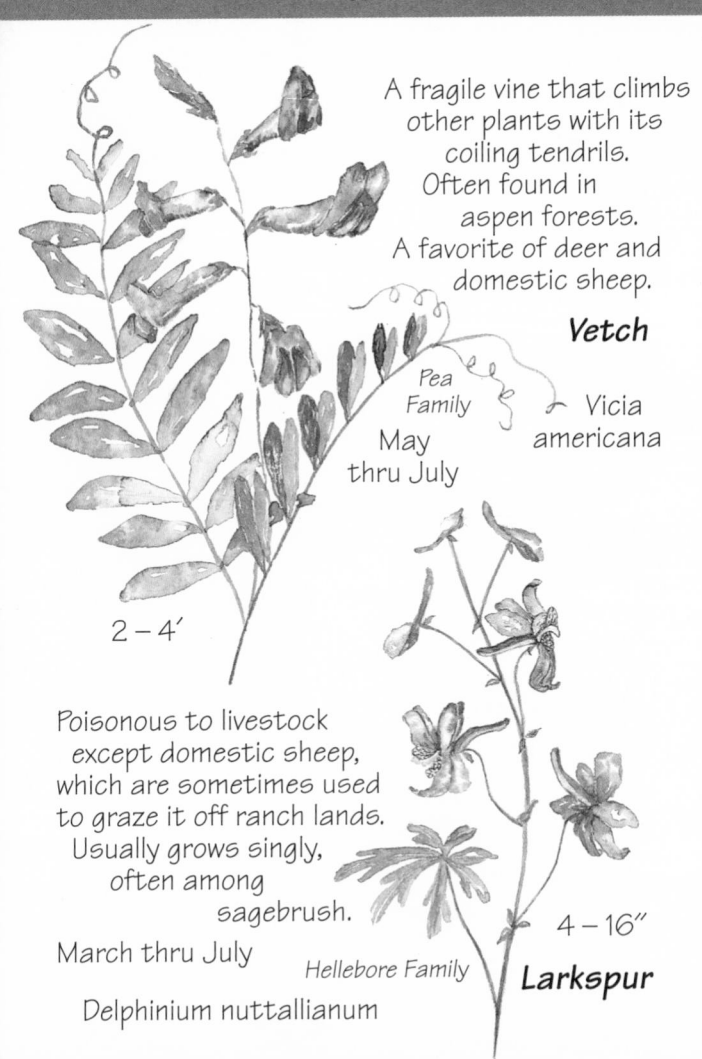

A fragile vine that climbs
other plants with its
coiling tendrils.
Often found in
aspen forests.
A favorite of deer and
domestic sheep.

Vetch

*Pea
Family*
May
thru July

Vicia
americana

2 – 4′

Poisonous to livestock
except domestic sheep,
which are sometimes used
to graze it off ranch lands.
Usually grows singly,
often among
sagebrush.

March thru July

Hellebore Family

4 – 16″

Larkspur

Delphinium nuttallianum

Often large patches grow by streams & in low wet meadows. Sometimes holes are dug near irises to fill up with water for livestock.

Iris

Known as "Blue Flag." Beautiful but poisonous. Close relative of the garden variety.

May thru July

8 – 20"

Iris Family

Iris missouriensis

References

Benedict, Audrey DeLella. *A Sierra Club Naturalist's Guide: The Southern Rockies*. San Francisco: Sierra Club Books, 1991.

Craighead, John J.; Craighead, Frank C. Jr.; and Davis, Ray J. *A Field Guide to Rocky Mountain Wildflowers*. The Peterson Field Guide Series. Boston: Houghton Mifflin Company, 1963.

Duft, Joseph F. and Moseley, Robert K. *Alpine Wildflowers of the Rocky Mountains*. Missoula, Montana: Mountain Press Publishing, 1989.

Guennel, G.K. *Guide to Colorado Wildflowers: Mountains*. Englewood, Colorado: Westcliffe Publishers, 1995.

_____. *Guide to Colorado Wildflowers: Plains & Foothills*. Englewood, Colorado: Westcliffe Publishers, 1995.

Jones, Charlotte Foltz. *Colorado Wildflowers*. Helena, Montana: Falcon Publishing, 1994.

Kershaw, Linda; MacKinnon, Andy; and Pojar, Jim. *Plants of the Rocky Mountains*. Renton, Washington: Lone Pine Publishing, 1998.

Newcomb, Lawrence. *Newcomb's Wildflower Guide*. New York: Little, Brown and Company, 1977.

Orr, Robert T. and Orr, Margaret C. *Wildflowers of Western America*. New York: Alfred A. Knopf, 1974.

Spellenberg, Richard. *The Audubon Society Field Guide to North American Wildflowers, Western Region*. New York: Alfred A. Knopf, 1979.

Strickler, Dee. *Alpine Wildflowers*. Columbia Falls, Montana: Flower Press, 1990.

_____. *Forest Wildflowers*. Columbia Falls, Montana: Flower Press, 1988.

Taylor, Ronald J. *Rocky Mountain Wildflowers*. Seattle: The Mountaineers, 1986.

Index